WESTMINSTER

SHORTER CATECHISM

COPYBOOK

Traditional Manuscript with Ruled Lines

Manuscript Writing Models

To the Teacher/Parent:

The text of the Westminster Catechism has been printed in manuscript as an example for the student.

For those questions that have longer answers, two copies have been included. The student may copy half of the text one day and finish the next.

For the older student, you may have them copy the questions and answers as well. For the younger student, the answers alone may be sufficient.

Additional copies of this text may be purchased at
www.brookdalehouse.com

Also available at Brookdale House:

The Write from History Series
(A history based classical writing program for students in grades 1 through 5, covering the four year history cycle. Available in both manuscript and cursive.)

The Westminster Shorter Catechism Copybook
(Available in traditional, modern, vertical, and italic cursive.)

The Fun Spanish level 1

Sheldon's New Primary Language Lessons
(A gentle introduction to grammar and composition for elementary students)

Q1: What is the chief end of man?

A1: Man's chief end is to glorify God and to enjoy him forever.

Q2: What rule hath God given to direct us how we may glorify and enjoy him?

A2: The Word of God, which is contained in the Scriptures of the Old and New Testaments, is the only rule to direct us how we may glorify and enjoy him.

Q3:   What do the Scriptures
        principally teach?

A3:   The Scriptures principally teach
        what man is to believe concerning
        God, and what duty God requires
        of man.

Q4: What is God?

A4: God is a Spirit, infinite, eternal, and unchangeable, in his being, wisdom, power, holiness, justice, goodness, and truth.

Q5: Are there more Gods than one?

A5: There is but one only, the living and true God.

Q6: How many persons are there in the Godhead?

A6: There are three persons in the Godhead; the Father, the Son, and the Holy Ghost; and these three are one God, the same in substance, equal in power and glory.

Q7: What are the decrees of God?

A7: The decrees of God are, his eternal purpose, according to the counsel of his will, hereby, for his own glory, he has foreordained whatsoever comes to pass.

Q8: How doth God execute his decrees?

A8: God executeth his decrees in the works of creation and providence.

Q9: What is the work of creation?

A9: The work of creation is God's making all things of nothing, by the word of his power, in the space of six days, and all very good.

Q10: How did God create man?

A10: God created man male and female, after his own image, in knowledge, righteousness, and holiness, with dominion over the creatures.

Q11: What are God's works of providence?

A11: God's works of providence are, his most holy, wise, and powerful preserving and governing all his creatures, and all their actions.

_____

Q12: What special act of providence did God exercise toward man in the estate wherein he was created?

A12: When God had created man, he entered into a covenant of life with him, upon condition of perfect obedience; forbidding him to eat of the tree of the knowledge of good and evil, upon the pain of death.

Q13: Did our first parents continue in the estate wherein they were created?

A13: Our first parents, being left to the freedom of their own will, fell from the estate wherein they were created, by sinning against God.

Q14:   What is sin?

A14:   Sin is any want of conformity unto, or transgression of, the law of God.

Q15: What was the sin whereby our first parents fell from the estate wherein they were created?

A15: The sin whereby our first parents fell from the estate wherein they were created, was their eating the forbidden fruit.

Q16: Did all mankind fall in Adam's first transgression?

A16: The covenant being made with Adam, not only for himself, but for his posterity; all mankind, descending from him by ordinary generation, sinned in him, and fell with him, in his first transgression.

Q17:   Into what estate did the fall bring mankind?

A17:   The fall brought mankind into an estate of sin and misery.

Q18: Wherein consists the sinfulness of that estate whereinto man fell?

A18: The sinfulness of that estate whereinto man fell consists in the guilt of Adam's first sin, the want of original righteousness, and the corruption of his whole nature, which is commonly called Original Sin; together with all actual transgressions which proceed from it.

Q19:   What is the misery of that estate whereinto man fell?

A19:   All mankind by their fall lost communion with God, are under his wrath and curse, and so made liable to all miseries in this life, to death itself, and to the pains of hell for ever.

Q20: Did God leave all mankind to perish in the estate of sin and misery?

A20: God, having, out of his mere good pleasure, from all eternity, elected some to everlasting life, did enter into a covenant of grace, to deliver them out of the estate of sin and misery, and to bring them into an estate of salvation by a Redeemer.

Q21:   Who is the Redeemer of God's elect?

A21:   The only Redeemer of God's elect is the Lord Jesus Christ, who, being the eternal Son of God, became man, and so was, and continueth to be, God and man in two distinct natures, and one person, forever.

Q22: How did Christ, being the Son of God, become man?

A22: Christ, the Son of God, became man, by taking to himself a true body, and a reasonable soul, being conceived by the power of the Holy Ghost, in the womb of the Virgin Mary, and born of her, yet without sin.

Q23: What offices doth Christ execute as our Redeemer?

A23: Christ, as our Redeemer, executeth the offices of a prophet, of a priest, and of a king, both in his estate of humiliation and exaltation.

Q24: How doth Christ execute the office of a prophet?

A24: Christ executeth the office of a prophet, in revealing to us, by his word and Spirit, the will of God for our salvation.

Q25:   How doth Christ execute the
       office of a priest?

A25:   Christ executeth the office of a
       priest, in his once offering up of
       himself a sacrifice to satisfy
       divine justice, and in his reconciling
       us to God, and in his making
       continual intercession for us.

Q26: How doth Christ execute the office of a king?

A26: Christ executes the office of a king, in subduing us to himself, in ruling and defending us, and in restraining and conquering all his and our enemies.

Q27: Wherein did Christ's humiliation consist?

A27: Christ's humiliation consisted in his being born, and that in a low condition, made under the law, undergoing the miseries of this life, the wrath of God, and the cursed death of the cross; in being buried, and continuing under the power of death for a time.

Q28: Wherein consisteth Christ's exaltation?

A28: Christ's exaltation consisteth in his rising again from the dead on the third day, in ascending up into heaven, in sitting at the right hand of God the Father, and in coming to judge the world at the last day.

Q29:   How are we made partakers of the redemption purchased by Christ?

A29:   We are made partakers of the redemption purchased by Christ, by the effectual application of it to us by his Holy Spirit.

Q30:   How doth the Spirit apply to us the redemption purchased by Christ?

A30:   The Spirit applieth to us the redemption purchased by Christ, by working faith in us, and thereby uniting us to Christ in our effectual calling.

Q31: What is effectual calling?

A31: Effectual calling is the work of God's Spirit, whereby convincing us of our sin and misery, enlightening our minds in the knowledge of Christ, and renewing our wills, he doth persuade and enable us to embrace Jesus Christ, freely offered to us in the gospel.

Q32:   What benefits do they that are effectually called partake of in this life?

A32:   They that are effectually called do in this life partake of justification, adoption, and sanctification, and the several benefits which, in this life, do either accompany or flow from them.

Q33:   What is justification?

A33:   Justification is an act of God's free grace, wherein he pardoneth all our sins and accepteth us as righteous in his sight, only for the righteousness of Christ imputed to us, and received by faith alone.

Q34: What is adoption?

A34: Adoption is an act of God's free grace, whereby we are received into the number, and have a right to all the privileges of the Sons of God.

Q35:   What is sanctification?

A35:   Sanctification is the work of God's free grace, whereby we are renewed in the whole man after the image of God, and are enabled more and more to die unto sin, and live unto righteousness.

Q36: What are the benefits which in this life do accompany or flow from justification, adoption, and sanctification?

A36: The benefits which in this life do accompany or flow from justification, adoption, and sanctification, are, assurance of God's love, peace of conscience, joy in the Holy Ghost, increase of grace, and perseverance therein to the end.

Q37:   What benefits do believers receive from Christ at death?

A37:   The souls of believers are at their death made perfect in holiness, and do immediately pass into glory; and their bodies, being still united to Christ, do rest in their graves till the resurrection.

Q38: What benefits do believers receive from Christ at the resurrection?

A38: At the resurrection, believers being raised up in glory, shall be openly acknowledged and acquitted in the day of judgement, and made perfectly blessed in the full enjoying of God to all eternity.

Q39: What is the duty which God requireth of man?

A39: The duty which God requireth of man is obedience to his revealed will.

Q40: What did God at first reveal to man for the rule of his obedience?

A40: The rule, which God at first revealed to man for his obedience, was the Moral Law.

Q41: Wherein is the Moral Law summarily comprehended?

A41: The Moral Law is summarily comprehended in the Ten Commandments.

Q42: What is the sum of the Ten Commandments?

A42: The sum of the Ten Commandments is, "to love the Lord our God" with all our heart, with all our soul, with all our strength, and with all our mind, and our neighbor as ourselves.

Q43:   What is the preface to the Ten Commandments?

A43:   The preface to the Ten Commandments is in these words, "I am the Lord your God, who brought you out of the land of Egypt, out of the house of slavery."

Q44:   What doth the preface to the Ten Commandments teach us?

A44:   The preface to the Ten Commandments teacheth us, that because God is The Lord, our God, and Redeemer; therefore we are bound to keep all his commandments.

Q45: Which is the First Commandment?

A45: The First Commandment is, "Thou shalt have no other gods before me."

Q46:   What is requireth in the First Commandment?

A46:   The First Commandment requires us to know and acknowledge God to be the only true God, and our God; and to worship and glorify him accordingly.

Q47:   What is forbidden in the First Commandment?

A47:   The First Commandment forbiddeth the denying, or not worshipping and glorifying the true God, as God, and our God, and the giving of that worship and glory to any other which is due to him alone.

Q48:   What are we specially taught by these words, "before me" in the First Commandment?

A48:   These words "before me" in the First Commandment, teach us, that God who seeth all things, taketh notice of, and is much displeased with, the sin of having any other God.

Q49: Which is the Second Commandment?

A49: The Second Commandment is, "Thou shall not make unto thee any graven image, or any likeness of any thing that is in heaven above, or that is in the earth beneath, or that is in the water under the earth, thou shalt not bow down thyself to them, nor serve them: for I the Lord thy God am a jealous God, visiting the iniquity of the fathers upon the children, unto the third and fourth generation of them that hate me ; and showing mercy unto thousands of them that love me , and keep my commandments."

Q49: Which is the Second Commandment?

A49: The Second Commandment is, "Thou shall not make unto thee any graven image, or any likeness of any thing that is in heaven above, or that is in the earth beneath, or that is in the water under the earth, thou shalt not bow down thyself to them, nor serve them: for I the Lord thy God am a jealous God, visiting the iniquity of the fathers upon the children, unto the third and fourth generation of them that hate me ; and showing mercy unto thousands of them that love me , and keep my commandments."

Q50:   What is required in the Second Commandment?

A50:   The Second Commandment requireth the receiving, observing, and keeping pure and entire, all such religious worship and ordinances as God hath appointed in his Word.

Q51: What is forbidden in the Second Commandment?

A51: The Second Commandment forbiddeth the worshipping of God by images, or any other way not appointed in his Word.

Q52: What are the reasons annexed to the Second Commandment?

A52: The reasoned annexed to the Second Commandment are, God's sovereignty over us, and the zeal he hath to his own worship.

Q53: Which is the Third Commandment?

A53: The Third Commandment is, "Thou shalt not take the name of the Lord thy God in vain: for the Lord will not hold him guiltless that taketh his name in vain."

Q54: What is required in the Third Commandment?

A54: The Third Commandment requireth the holy and reverent use of God's names, titles, attributes, ordinances, Word, and works.

Q55: What is forbidden in the Third Commandment?

A55: The Third Commandment forbiddeth all profaning or abusing anything whereby God maketh himself known.

Q56: What is the reason annexed to the Third Commandment?

A56: The reason annexed to the Third Commandment is, that however the breakers of this commandment may escape punishment from men, yet the Lord our God will not suffer them to escape his righteous judgement.

Q57:   Which is the Fourth Commandment?

A57:   The Fourth Commandment is, "Remember the Sabbath-day, to keep it holy: Six days shalt thou labor, and do all thy work: but the seventh day is the Sabbath of the Lord thy God:in it thou shalt not do any work, thou, nor thy son, nor thy daughter, thy manservant, nor thy maid-servant, nor thy cattle, nor thy stranger that is within thy gates: For in six days the Lord made heaven and earth, the sea, and all that is in them, and rested the seventh day:wherefore the Lord blessed the Sabbath day, and hallowed it."

Q57: Which is the Fourth Commandment?

A57: The Fourth Commandment is, "Remember the Sabbath-day, to keep it holy: Six days shalt thou labor, and do all thy work: but the seventh day is the Sabbath of the Lord thy God: in it thou shalt not do any work, thou, nor thy son, nor thy daughter, thy manservant, nor thy maid-servant, nor thy cattle, nor thy stranger that is within thy gates: For in six days the Lord made heaven and earth, the sea, and all that is in them, and rested the seventh day: wherefore the Lord blessed the Sabbath day, and hallowed it."

Q58: What is required in the Fourth Commandment?

A58: The Fourth Commandment requireth the keeping holy to God such set times as he appointed in his Word, expressly one whole day in seven to be a holy Sabbath to himself.

Q59:   Which day of the seven hath God
        appointed to be the weekly
        Sabbath?

A59:   From the beginning of the world to
        the resurrection of Christ, God
        appointed the seventh day of the
        week to be the weekly Sabbath;
        and the first day of the week ever
        since, to continue to the end of
        the world, which is the Christian
        Sabbath.

Q60:   How is the Sabbath to be sanctified?

A60:   The Sabbath is to be sanctified by a holy resting all that day, even from such worldly employments and recreations as are lawful on other days; and spending the whole time in the public and private exercises of God's worship, except so much as is to be taken up in the works of necessity and mercy.

Q61:   What is forbidden in the Fourth Commandment?

A61:   The Fourth Commandment forbiddeth the omission or careless performance of the duties required and the profaning the day by idleness, or doing that which is in itself sinful, or by unnecessary thoughts, words, or works about our worldly employments or recreations.

Q62: What are the reasons annexed to the Fourth Commandment?

A62: The reasons annexed to the Fourth Commandment are, God's allowing us six days of the week for our own employments, his challenging a special propriety in the seventh, his own example, and his blessing the Sabbath day.

Q63:   Which is the Fifth
        Commandment?

A63:   The Fifth Commandment is,
        "Honor thy father and thy mother,
        that thy days may be long upon the
        land which the Lord thy God
        giveth thee."

Q64:   What is required in the Fifth Commandment?

A64:   The Fifth Commandment requireth preserving the honor and performing the duties belonging to every one in their several places and relations as superiors, inferiors, or equals.

Q65: What is the forbidden in the Fifth Commandment?

A65: The Fifth Commandment forbiddeth the neglecting of, or doing anything against, the honor and duty which belongeth to every one in their several places and relations.

Q66: What is the reason annexed to the Fifth Commandment?

A66: The reason annexed to the Fifth Commandment is a promise of long life and prosperity (as far as it shall serve for God's glory and their own good) to all such as keep this commandment.

Q67:   Which is the Sixth
       Commandment?

A67:   The Sixth Commandment is, "Thou
       shalt not kill."

Q68: What is required in the Sixth Commandment?

A68: The Sixth Commandment requireth all lawful endeavors to preserve our own life, and the life of others.

Q69: What is forbidden in the Sixth Commandment?

A69: The Sixth Commandment forbiddeth the taking away of our own life, or the life of our neighbor unjustly, or whatsoever tendeth thereunto.

Q70: Which is the Seventh Commandment?

A70: The Seventh Commandment is, "Thou shalt not commit adultery."

_____
_____
_____
_____
_____
_____
_____
_____
_____
_____
_____
_____
_____
_____
_____
_____
_____
_____

Q71: What is required in the Seventh Commandment?

A71: The Seventh Commandment requireth the preservation of our own and our neighbor's chastity, in heart, speech, and behavior.

Q72: What is forbidden in the Seventh Commandment?

A72: The Seventh Commandment forbiddeth all unchaste thoughts, words, and actions.

Q73: Which is the Eighth Commandment?

A73: The Eighth Commandment is, "Thou shalt not steal."

_____
....
_____
_____
....
_____
_____
....
_____
_____
....
_____
_____
....
_____
_____
....
_____
_____
....
_____

Q74:   What is required in the Eighth Commandment?

A74:   The Eighth Commandment requireth the lawful procuring and furthering the wealth and outward estate of ourselves and others.

Q75: What is forbidden in the Eighth Commandment?

A75: The Eighth Commandment forbiddeth whatsoever doth or may unjustly hinder our own or our neighbor's wealth or outward estate.

Q76: What is the Ninth Commandment?

A76: The Ninth Commandment is, "Thou shalt not bear false witness against thy neighbor."

Q77:   What is required in the Ninth Commandment?

A77:   The Ninth Commandment requireth the maintaining and promoting of truth between man and man, and of our own and our neighbor's good name, especially in witness bearing.

Q78:   What is forbidden in the Ninth Commandment?

A78:   The Ninth Commandment forbiddeth whatsoever is prejudicial to truth or injurious to our own or our neighbor's good name.

Q79:   Which is the Tenth Commandment?

A79:   The Tenth Commandment is, "Thou shalt not covet thy neighbor's house, thou shall not covet thy neighbor's wife, nor his manservant, nor his maidservant, nor his ox, nor his ass, nor any thing that is thy neighbor's."

Q80: What is required in the Tenth Commandment?

A80: The Tenth Commandment requireth full contentment with our own condition, with a right and charitable frame of spirit toward our neighbor, and all this is his.

Q81:   What is forbidden in the Tenth Commandment?

A81:   The Tenth Commandment forbiddeth all discontentment with our own estate, envying or grieving at the good of our neighbor, and all inordinate motions and affections to any thing that is his.

Q82: Is any man able perfectly to keep the commandments of God?

A82: No mere man, since the fall, is able in this life to perfectly keep the commandments of God, but doth daily break them in thought, word, and deed.

Q83: Are all transgression of the law equally heinous?

A83: Some sins in themselves, and by reason of several aggravations, are more heinous in the sight of God than others.

Q84: What doth every sin deserve?

A84: Every sin deserveth God's wrath and curse, both in this life, and in that which is to come.

Q85: What doth God require of us, that we may escape his wrath and curse due to us for sin?

A85: To escape the wrath and curse of God due to us for sin, God requireth of us faith in Jesus Christ, repentance unto life, with the diligent use of all the outward means whereby Christ communicateth to us the benefits of redemption.

Q86: What is faith in Jesus Christ?

A86: Faith in Jesus Christ is a saving grace, whereby we receive and rest upon him alone for salvation, as he is offered to us in the gospel.

Q87:   What is repentance unto life?

A87:   Repentance unto life is a saving grace whereby a sinner, out of a true sense of his sin, and apprehension of the mercy of God in Christ, doth, with grief and hatred of his sin, turn from it unto God, with full purpose of, and endeavor after, new obedience.

Q88: What are the outward means whereby Christ communicateth to us the benefits of redemption?

A88: The outward and ordinary means whereby Christ communicateth to us the benefits of redemption, are his ordinances, especially the Word, sacraments, and prayer; all which are made effectual to the elect for salvation.

Q89: How is the Word made effectual to salvation?

A89: The Spirit of God maketh the reading, but especially the preaching of the Word, an effectual means of convincing and converting sinners, and of building them up in holiness and comfort, through faith, unto salvation.

Q90:   How is the Word to be read and heard that it may become effectual to salvation?

A90:   That the Word may become effectual to salvation, we must attend thereunto with diligence, preparation, and prayer; receive it with faith and love, lay it up in our hearts, and practice it in our lives.

Q91: How do the sacraments become effectual means of salvation?

A91: The sacraments become effectual means of salvation, not from any virtue in them nor in him that doth administer them but only by the blessing of Christ and the working of his Spirit in them that, by faith, receive them.

Q92:   What is a sacrament?

A92:   A sacrament is a holy ordinance
instituted by Christ, wherein, by
sensible signs, Christ, and the
benefits of the new covenant, are
represented, sealed, and applied to
believers.

Q93: Which are the sacraments of the New Testament?

A93: The sacraments of the New Testament are Baptism and the Lord's supper.

Q94:   What is baptism?

A94:   Baptism is a sacrament, wherein the washing with water in the name of the Father, and of the Son, and of the Holy Ghost, doth signify and seal our ingrafting into Christ, and partaking of the benefits of the covenant of grace, and our engagement to be the Lord's.

Q95: To whom is baptism to be administered?

A95: Baptism is not to be administered to any that are out of the visible church, till they profess their faith in Christ and obedience to him; but the infants of such as are members of the visible church are to be baptized.

Q96: What is the Lord's supper?

A96: The Lord's Supper is a sacrament, wherein, by giving and receiving bread and wine, according to Christ's appointment, his death is showed forth; and the worth receivers are, not after a corporal and carnal manner but by faith, made partakers of his body and blood with all his benefits to their spiritual nourishment and growth in grace.

Q97: What is required to be the worthy receiving of the Lord's supper?

A97: It is required of them that would worthily partake of the Lord's supper, that they examine themselves of their knowledge to discern the Lord's body, of their faith to feed upon him, of their repentance, love, and new obedience; lest, coming unworthily, they eat and drink judgement to themselves.

Q98: What is prayer?

A98: Prayer is an offering up of our desires unto God for things agreeable to his will, in the name of Christ, with confession of our sins, and thankful acknowledgement of his mercies.

Q99:   What rule hath God given for our direction in prayer?

A99:   The whole Word of God is of use to direct us in prayer; but the special rule of direction is that form of prayer which Christ taught his disciples, commonly called The Lord's Prayer.

Q100: What doth the preface of the Lord's prayer teach us?

A100: The preface of the Lord's prayer, which is, "Our Father which art in heaven," teacheth us to draw near to God with all holy reverence and confidence, as children to a father, able and ready to help us; and that we should pray with and for others.

Q101: What do we pray for in the first petition?

A101: In the first petition, which is, "Hallowed be thy name," we pray, that God would enable us and others to glorify him in all that whereby he maketh himself known; and that he would dispose all things to his own glory.

Q102: What do we pray for in the second petition?

A102: In the second petition, which is, "Thy kingdom come," we pray, that Satan's kingdom may be destroyed; and that the kingdom of grace may be advanced, ourselves and others brought into it, and kept in it; and the kingdom of glory may be hastened.

Q103: What do we pray for in the third petition?

A103: In the third petition, which is, "Thy will be done in earth, as it is in heaven," we pray, that God, by his grace, would make us able and willing to know, obey, and submit to his will in all things, as the angels do in heaven.

Q104: What do we pray for in the fourth petition?

A104: In the fourth petition, which is, "Give us this day our daily bread," we pray, that of God's free gift we may receive a competent portion of the good things of this life, and enjoy his blessing with them.

Q105: What do we pray for in the fifth petition?

A105: In the fifth petition, which is, "And forgive us our debts, as we forgive our debtors," we pray, that God, for Christ's sake, would freely pardon all our sins; which we are able to be rather encouraged to ask, because by his grace we are enabled from the heart to forgive others.

Q106: What do we pray for in the sixth petition?

A106: In the sixth petition, which is, "And lead us not into temptation, but deliver us from evil," we pray that God would either keep us from being tempted to sin, or support and deliver us when we are tempted.

Q107: What doth the conclusion of the Lord's prayer teach us?

A107: The conclusion of the Lord's prayer, which is, "For thine is the kingdom, and the power, and the glory, for ever, Amen." teacheth us, to take our encouragement in prayer from God only, and in our prayers to praise him, ascribing kingdom, power and glory to him.

And, in testimony of our desire, and assurance to be heard, we say, Amen.